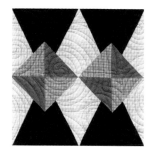

Twice as Nice

Quilts with Scrap-Saving
Bonus Projects

Kari M. Carr

Martingale
Create with Confidence

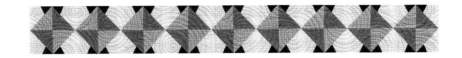

Twice as Nice:
Quilts with Scrap-Saving Bonus Projects
© 2012 by Kari M. Carr

Martingale®
19021 120th Ave. NE, Ste. 102
Bothell, WA 98011-9511 USA
ShopMartingale.com

Credits

President & CEO: Tom Wierzbicki

Editor in Chief: Mary V. Green

Design Director: Paula Schlosser

Managing Editor: Karen Costello Soltys

Technical Editor: Laurie Baker

Copy Editor: Melissa Bryan

Production Manager: Regina Girard

Illustrators: Missy Shepler & Adrienne Smitke

Cover & Text Designer: Regina Girard

Photographer: Brent Kane

Printed in China
17 16 15 14 13 12   8 7 6 5 4 3 2 1

Library of Congress Cataloging-in-Publication Data is available upon request.

ISBN: 978-1-60468-176-5

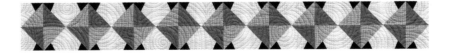

Contents

Introduction

Isn't it wonderful when you get more bang for your buck? Or when you don't just *have* good intentions but *actually finish* a quilt using your fabric scraps? You can accomplish both of these with the projects in *Twice as Nice!* And do you want to know the best part? The concept is so simple. Not only will you enjoy the main quilt projects, but you'll find the bonus projects, well, *nice!*

I don't know about you, but I have a whole stash of clipped fabric corner pieces that I keep telling myself I'm going to do something with. The thought of pinning together all those pieces and stitching on the bias just makes me cringe. And then I think about what I can do with them . . . and, well, the bag gets closed and shoved to the back of the closet once again.

Then it dawned on me—all those pieces don't have to be wasted and forgotten, or, for that matter, handled again. Why not stitch a second seam at the same time you're making the original project? I don't like drawing lines any more than you do, so by using two different seam guides (¼" and ⅝") on the Clearly Perfect Angles stitching template that I designed, we can kill those proverbial two birds with one stone— voilà! There are no lines to draw, no wasted fabric, and

no wasted time. You get the idea. Once the extra corners had their very own seams, they needed their own design. And the bonus project was created.

A goal for me when I write my books is to include a variety of projects, made in a variety of fabrics and styles. You'll find quilts with simple appliqué such as "Warm Welcome" (page 14) and "Liberty" (page 48); bright, chunky piecing in "Split Pea Soup" (page 21); and delicate prairie points on "Prairie Rose" (page 28). There is also a unique bed runner called "Heavenly Days" (page 36) and a quilt with some challenging angles, "To Sir, with Love" (page 56).

Because the main quilts display such variety, so, too, do the bonus projects. They range in size from small mug mats and a pincushion to a good-sized wall hanging.

You'll find all the information you need to use the Clearly Perfect Angle tool for quick and accurate triangles, as well as step-by-step instructions for making the projects in this book. However, if you need any assistance with how to apply binding, or measure for borders, or even the basics of rotary cutting, please visit ShopMartingale.com/HowtoQuilt and download free illustrated information on many different quilt-making topics.

Nice is good, but *twice as nice* is even better! Enjoy!

I consider myself a practical person, as you can tell from the introduction to this book. So when my precious sewing time was being used to draw lines for making half-square triangles, or sewing through and then ripping away paper, I was very frustrated. And I sure thought it was impractical to have sticky, gummy tape on my machine. I just knew there had to be a better way!

While at a retreat, I noticed a ruler on my sewing table that stayed in place with static cling. A lightbulb went on in my head at that moment, and the Clearly Perfect Angles (CPA) stitching template was born. Tens of thousands of quilters now know how accurately and efficiently they can sew 45° angles without marking their fabric, ripping away paper, or having that yucky tape on their machine.

Following is an overview of three techniques I used for the projects in this book involving the Clearly Perfect Angles stitching template. It's important to learn each of these methods so you'll be satisfied with your finished projects. Once you've learned the techniques, you'll appreciate the simplicity and accuracy of sewing 45° angles. For video demonstrations of these techniques and more, as well as how to properly apply the CPA to your sewing machine, I invite you to visit my website at NewLeafStitches.com. If you have a smart phone, you can use the QR code below to go there.

Anatomy of the Clearly Perfect Angles

Let's begin with a closer look at the Clearly Perfect Angles template for a better understanding of how the techniques work.

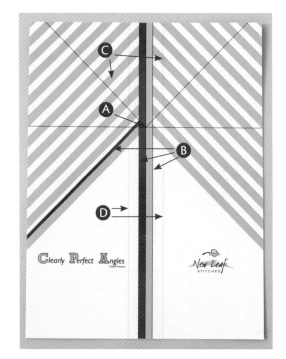

A. Position of the sewing-machine needle.

B. ¼" seam guides on both sides of the center. The green vertical band is most commonly used for sewing accurate ¼" seams. The dark-gray vertical band is used in conjunction with the angled dark-gray band.

C. Angled green bands are used together for fabric alignment with any of the techniques.

D. ⅝" seam guide on both sides of the center. Originally included for garment making, I've used these lines exclusively for sewing the bonus units for the projects in this book.

Basic Center Alignment

This is the method used for basic half-square-triangle units (shown in the photos on page 8), Flying Geese blocks, Snowball blocks, and any angle that is sewn diagonally from point to point. The center alignment is also used for joining border or binding strips. Before you begin, apply the CPA to your sewing machine and sewing table as instructed on the package insert.

Stitching from Point to Point

1. With right sides together and raw edges of the fabric pieces aligned as directed in the project instructions, position the pieces so that one corner point is at the needle and the opposite corner point is on the thin black vertical centerline between the gray and green vertical lines on the CPA. If your bottom point extends farther than the centerline on the template, see "Angled Green Band Alignment" on page 11.

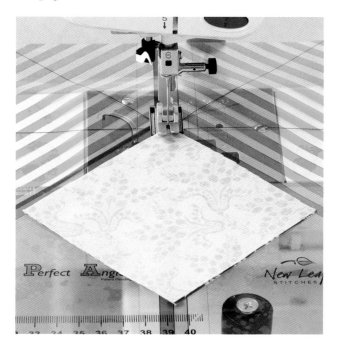

2. Stitch diagonally across the pieces, keeping the bottom point on the centerline.

3. Trim the seam allowances to ¼".

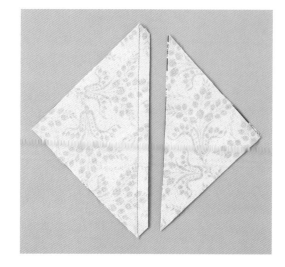

4. Press open the piece, directing the seam allowances as instructed for the project.

Joining Border and Binding Strips

1. With right sides together, overlap two strips at a right angle, creating inverted points that will be used to follow the guidelines on the CPA.

2. Place one inverted point at the needle and the opposite inverted point on the thin black centerline as a guide. Stitch diagonally across the strips, keeping the bottom inverted point on the centerline.

3. Trim the seam allowances to ¼".

4. Press the seam allowances as instructed for the project. Your strips are perfectly joined and the seam is hardly noticeable!

Gray Band Alignment

I wanted the Clearly Perfect Angle tool to be user friendly, so I color coded it for easy alignment with various techniques. Use the vertical and angled *gray* bands when instructed to sew ¼" from each side of the points on a pair of squares to make two half-square-triangle units.

1. With right sides together and raw edges matching, align the squares so that the top point is to the left of the needle, the upper-left edge is aligned with the top edge of the *angled* gray band, and the bottom point is aligned with the outside edge of the *vertical* gray band (which is ¼" from the center needle position). If your bottom point extends farther than the gray band on the template, see "Angled Green Band Alignment" on page 11.

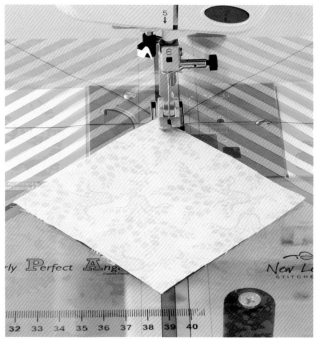

Seam Guides
Most people leave the Clearly Perfect Angles template in place all the time, using the conveniently provided seam guides for all their sewing projects.

2. Stitch diagonally across the squares, keeping the bottom point on the outside of the *vertical* gray band.

3. Rotate the squares and repeat the stitching process on the opposite side of the points.

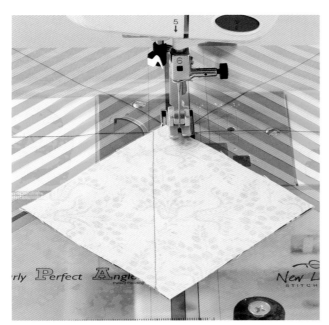

4. Cut the squares apart from point to point between the two stitching lines.

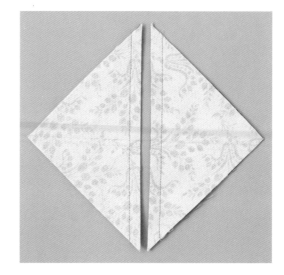

5. Press open the squares, directing the seam allowances as instructed for the project.

Chain Piecing

Chain piecing is quick and easy using the Clearly Perfect Angles template. Simply use it for any of the techniques.

Angled Green Band Alignment

Rely on the angled green bands to help you align large squares of fabric while using either one of the first two techniques. For example, your fabric squares may be larger than the original size of the Clearly Perfect Angles template (see "Heavenly Days" on page 36). Or, you may have an instance in which your sewing area is shallower than the CPA and you lose some length. This is one of the reasons the CPA is so user friendly; it can be customized to your particular sewing setup.

Stitching from Point to Point

1. Layer your fabric squares, right sides together. Position the pieces so that the top corner point is at the needle. You'll notice that when the point is at the needle, the square is too large for the opposite corner point to have any line to follow. You'll need to align the upper edges of the squares with the green angled bands.

2. *Slowly* begin stitching, watching the fabric and template *angled* edges so that they keep the same angle at all times. Move through the green and clear angled areas until your bottom corner point has a line to follow.

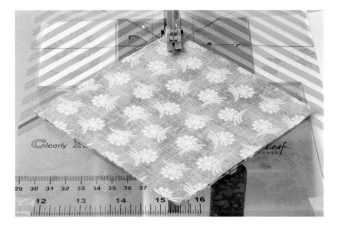

3. Follow the centerline to finish stitching through the squares.

Stitching ¼" from the Points

1. Layer your squares right sides together and place them on the CPA as described for gray band alignment (page 9). Notice that the angles will be the same; however, when one side of your fabric is at a *green* portion of the angled band, the opposite side will be at the *clear* portion of the angled band.

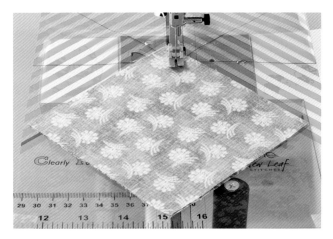

2. *Slowly* begin stitching, watching the fabric and template *angled* edges so that they keep the same alignment at all times. When you have sewn through enough of the square to see the vertical gray band at the bottom of the template, align the bottom point of the squares with the outside edge of the vertical gray band and continue stitching through the squares.

3. Rotate the squares and repeat the stitching process on the opposite side of the points.

Making the Bonus Units

Creating the bonus units from squares that have been sewn together point to point is very simple. This technique is an easy way to utilize excess fabric on any quilting project, not just the ones in this book. Let's get started.

1. After you've finished sewing your squares diagonally from point to point, *do not* trim the seam allowances to ¼". Instead, move the squares to the left so that the top and bottom points are lined up with the ⅝" dotted line on the Clearly Perfect Angles template.

2. Stitch a second seam ⅝" from the original seam, following the dotted line. Then cut the squares apart between the two stitching lines. The seam allowances will be slightly larger than ¼".

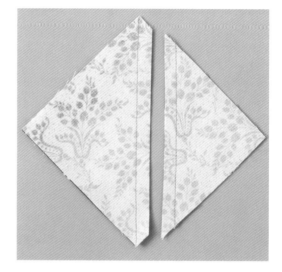

3. Press the seam allowances open unless otherwise directed.

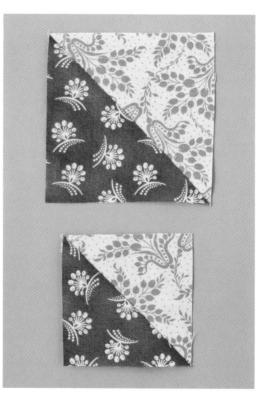

Tips for Successful Bonus Projects

- Use starch! Some of the pieces get pretty small, but starching your fabric will help the pieces hold their shape.
- Maintaining a ¼" seam allowance is *very* important. If your main project is done accurately, your bonus units will be accurate as well.
- Chain piecing is efficient. After chain stitching the main squares together, go back and do your stitching for the bonus units. When cutting between the stitching lines, don't clip the threads of the bonus pieces. It's easier to keep track of them when they're chained together.

- Be careful when trimming down the pieces so that the angles are maintained and you don't lose any points.
- Press all the seam allowances open . . . it will preserve your sanity.
- If you're saving the pieces for later, label which project they're for.
- With the exception of backing and binding, the yardage requirements listed for the main project will be enough to complete the bonus project.

Warm Welcome

I designed this wool-appliqué wall hanging for my kitchen, and it was just too cute not to share. With it, I'm sending warm wishes from my home to yours.

Finished Wall Hanging: 12½" x 15½" • Finished Center Block: 8" x 11"

Pieced and quilted by Kari Carr

Materials

Wool fabrics don't have to be felted, but they should be tightly woven.

Fat quarter (18" x 22") of green-print cotton for border and binding

Fat quarter of black-print cotton for center background and border

Fat eighth (9" x 22") of red-print cotton for border

Fat eighth of gold-print cotton for flange

10" x 10" square of red wool for pineapple appliqué background and letter appliqués

6" x 6" square of green wool for leaf appliqués

5" x 5" square of gold wool for pineapple appliqué

Fat quarter of fabric for backing

15" x 18" piece of batting

Lightweight fusible web for appliqués

Chalk pencil

Green floss or pearl cotton

Size 8 embroidery needle

Clearly Perfect Angles template

> The metal stand shown in the photo is from Ackfeld Manufacturing. For more information, contact the company at 1-888-272-3135 or visit the website at AckfeldWire.com.

Cutting

From the black print, cut:

2 strips, 3" x 18"; crosscut into 8 squares, 3" x 3"

1 rectangle, 10" x 13"

From the gold print, cut:

2 strips, 1" x 22"; crosscut *each strip* into:
- 1 rectangle, 1" x 9" (2 total)
- 1 rectangle, 1" x 12" (2 total)

From the green print, cut:

2 strips, 3" x 22"; crosscut into 8 squares, 3" x 3"

3 strips, 1¼" x 22"

From the red print, cut:

3 strips, 2½" x 22"; crosscut into:
- 16 squares, 2½" x 2½"
- 2 rectangles, 2½" x 7½"

Appliquéing the Center Block

This block uses fusible appliqué; for more details on preparing shapes for fusible appliqué, visit ShopMartingale.com/HowtoQuilt to download free illustrated how-to instructions.

1. From the red wool, cut a 6" x 10" rectangle. Set this rectangle aside for step 3.
2. Using the patterns on page 20 and the lightweight fusible web, prepare the pineapple and leaf appliqués from the fabrics indicated and the letter appliqués from the remainder of the red wool from step 1. Remove the paper backing from the fusible web on each piece.

3. Place the prepared pineapple appliqué pieces on the red-wool rectangle, referring to the pattern and the photo as necessary. Fuse and then hand whipstitch the pieces in place with matching thread. I recommend a 50-weight thread for appliquéing.

4. Thread your embroidery needle with three strands of green floss. Use a running stitch to add the detail work to the pineapple. In the spaces indicated on the pattern, make French knots.

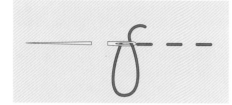

Running stitch

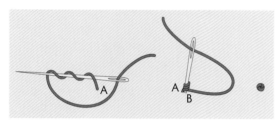

French knot

5. On the back of the red-wool rectangle, apply a piece of fusible web large enough to cover the appliqué work (approximately 5" x 9½"). Remove the paper backing. Carefully cut around the appliqué work so that approximately ⅛" of red wool is showing.

6. Using the chalk pencil, center and mark a 7½" x 10½" rectangle on the right side of the black-print rectangle to indicate the appliqué area. I like to cut my background fabric a little larger than necessary to allow for the distortion and fraying that can happen in the appliqué process. Then I trim it to size once the appliqués have been stitched in place.

7. Position the pineapple and letter appliqués within the chalked area. When you're satisfied with the placement, fuse the pieces in place. Hand whipstitch the wool pieces to the background using thread that matches the red wool.

8. Trim ½" from the chalk lines so that the block measures 8½" x 11½".

Attaching the Flange

1. Press each of the gold-print rectangles in half lengthwise, wrong sides together.

2. With the raw edges aligned, center and baste the longer folded rectangles to the sides of the appliquéd block; you'll have excess length extending beyond the block edges. Trim the ends of the rectangles even with the top and bottom edges of the

block. Baste the shorter folded rectangles to the top and bottom edges of the block in the same manner. Trim the ends of the rectangles even with the sides of the block.

Making the Borders

Here's what you need:

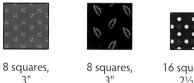

8 squares,
3"

8 squares,
3"

16 squares,
2½"

1. Layer each green 3" square with a black 3" square, right sides together. Stitch diagonally across each pair of squares, ¼" from each side of the points using the gray band alignment (page 9) on the Clearly Perfect Angles template (CPA). Cut the squares apart between the two stitching lines. Press the seam allowances open. Trim each half-square-triangle unit to 2½" x 2½".

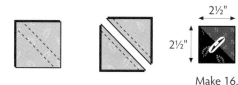

2½"

2½"

Make 16.

2. Layer each unit from step 1 with a red 2½" square, right sides together, with the black half of the unit from step 1 in the lower-left corner and the green half in the upper-right corner. Stitch diagonally from corner to corner as shown, using the basic center alignment (page 7) on the CPA. Stitch ⅝" from the first stitching line as shown, aligning the corners of the squares with the dotted seam guide on the CPA (page 12).

3. Cut the squares apart between the stitching lines. Press the seam allowances open. Trim the larger units to 2½" x 2½". Reserve the smaller units for the bonus project.

2½"

2½"

Make 16.

Make 16.
Reserve for
bonus project.

4. Join six large units from step 3 as shown to make the top border strip. Press the seam allowances open. Repeat to make the bottom border strip. These strips should measure 2½" x 12½".

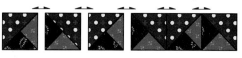

Make 2.

5. Join two of the remaining units from step 3 to the ends of a red 2½" x 7½" rectangle, watching color placement, to make the side border strip. Press the seam allowances toward the red rectangle. Repeat to make a total of two side border strips. These strips should measure 2½" x 11½".

Make 2.

6. Add the side borders to the sides of the center block as shown. Press the seam allowances toward the borders. Add the top and bottom border strips to the top and bottom edges of the quilt as shown. Press the seam allowances toward the borders.

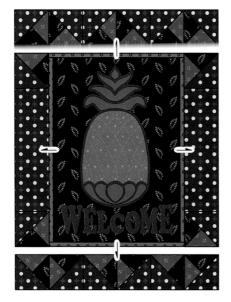

Quilt assembly

Finishing

For additional information on how to finish a quilt, including layering, basting, quilting, binding, and more, go to ShopMartingale.com/HowtoQuilt for free downloadable instructions.

Because of the small size of this quilt, I used 1¼"-wide strips and a single-fold technique to add the green binding. The only difference from the French double-fold binding method described in the downloadable instructions is that you don't press the joined strip in half lengthwise. Once you have the binding stitched to the quilt top, turn under the remaining raw edge ¼". Fold the binding over the quilt edge and stitch it to the back of the quilt. Reserve the remaining green strips for the bonus project.

BONUS PROJECT:

Welcome Mats

Savor these charming mug mats while you sip a warm cup of coffee or tea. You'll be able to make four mats from your leftover bonus units, so invite a friend or two over to enjoy them with you.

Finished Mug Mat: 4" x 4"

Materials

16 reserved bonus units from "Warm Welcome" (page 14)
Leftover gold-print and green-print cottons from "Warm Welcome"
12" x 12" square of fabric for backing
12" x 12" square of batting

Cutting

From the remaining gold print, cut:
8 rectangles, 1¼" x 2½"
8 rectangles, 1¼" x 4"

From the remaining green print, cut:
4 strips, 1¼" x 22"

Making the Mug Mats

1. Press the seam allowances of the reserved bonus units open. Square up the units to 1½" x 1½", making sure all the outside points end at the corners.

Make 16.

2. Arrange the bonus units into two rows of two units each as shown. Sew the units in each row together. Press the seam allowances open. Sew the rows together. Press the seam allowances open. The Pinwheel block should measure 2½" x 2½". Repeat to make a total of four Pinwheel blocks.

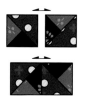

Make 4.

3. Sew gold 1¼" x 2½" rectangles to the top and bottom of each Pinwheel block. Press the seam allowances toward the gold rectangles. Join gold 1¼" x 4" rectangles to the sides of each block. Press the seam allowances toward the gold rectangles. The blocks should measure 4" x 4".

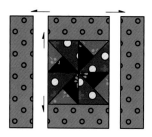

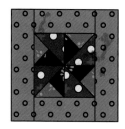

Make 4.

Finishing

For additional information on how to finish a quilt, including layering, basting, quilting, binding, and more, go to ShopMartingale.com/HowtoQuilt for free downloadable instructions.

Because of the small size of these mug mats, I used 1¼"-wide strips and a single-fold technique to add the green binding. Refer to the main project for further instructions.

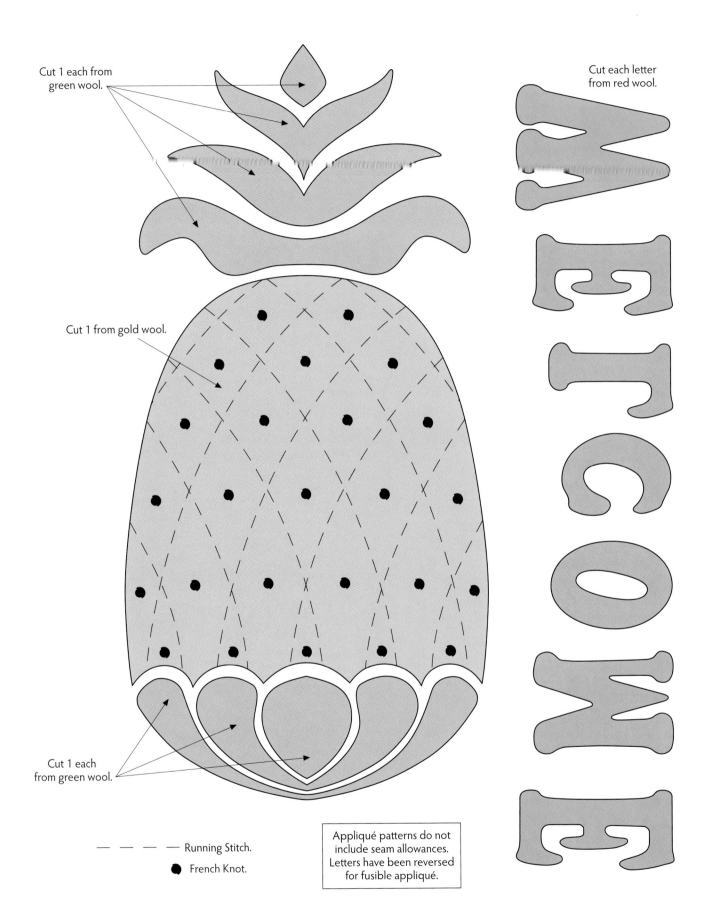

Cut 1 each from green wool.

Cut each letter from red wool.

Cut 1 from gold wool.

Cut 1 each from green wool.

— — — Running Stitch.
● French Knot.

Appliqué patterns do not include seam allowances. Letters have been reversed for fusible appliqué.

Split Pea Soup

There's nothing better than homemade soup.
Warm, hearty, and delicious . . . yum!

Finished Table Runner: 23½" x 53½" • Finished Block: 15" x 15"

Pieced by Kari Carr; quilted by Rosalie Davenport

Materials

Yardage is based on 42"-wide fabric.

1¼ yards of brown print for blocks, inner border, and binding

1 yard of gold print for block backgrounds

⅝ yard of green print for blocks and outer border

½ yard of blue print for blocks and outer border

Fat quarter (18" x 22") of red print for blocks

1¾ yards of fabric for backing

29" x 59" piece of batting

Clearly Perfect Angles template

Template plastic or Tri-Recs Tools

Cutting

If you aren't using the Tri-Recs Tools, trace the patterns on page 26 onto template plastic and cut them out.

From the green print, cut:

3 strips, 3½" x 42"; crosscut *1 of the strips* into 6 squares, 3½" x 3½". Cut the remainder of this strip in half crosswise and reserve the 2 pieces with the remaining 2 strips for the outer border.

1 strip, 4½" x 42"; crosscut into:
- 1 square, 4½" x 4½"
- 6 squares, 4" x 4"

From the blue print, cut:

2 strips, 3½" x 42"; crosscut into:
- 2 rectangles, 3½" x 17½"
- 6 squares, 3½" x 3½"

1 strip, 4½" x 42"; crosscut into:
- 1 square, 4½" x 4½"
- 6 squares, 4" x 4"

From the brown print, cut:

2 strips, 6½" x 42"; crosscut into 12 squares, 6½" x 6½"

3 strips, 1½" x 42"; crosscut *1 of the strips* into 2 strips, 1½" x 17½". Cut the remainder of this strip in half crosswise and reserve the 2 pieces with the remaining 2 strips for the inner border.

5 strips, 2¼" x 42"

2 squares, 4" x 4"

From the gold print, cut:

6 strips, 3½" x 42"; crosscut into:
- 36 squares, 3½" x 3½"
- 12 right-facing triangles and 12 left-facing triangles (24 triangles total) using the Tri-Recs Tool (at the 3½" line) **OR** the side triangle template

From the red print, cut:

2 strips, 3½" x 22"; crosscut into:
- 12 triangles using the Tri-Recs Tool (at the 3½" line) **OR** the center triangle template
- 3 squares, 3½" x 3½"

Making the Block Corner Units

Here's what you need:

6 squares,
4"

6 squares,
4"

36 squares,
3½"

12 squares,
6½"

1. Layer each green 4" square with a blue 4" square, right sides together. Stitch diagonally across each pair of squares, ¼" from each side of the points using the gray band alignment (page 9) on the Clearly Perfect Angles template (CPA). Cut the squares apart between the two stitching lines. Press the seam allowances toward the blue triangles. Trim each half-square-triangle unit to 3½" x 3½".

Make 12.

2. With right sides together, place gold squares on opposite corners of a brown square. Stitch diagonally from corner to corner as shown, using the basic center alignment (page 7) on the Clearly Perfect Angles template. Stitch ⅝" from the first stitching lines as shown, aligning the corners of the squares with the dotted seam guide on the CPA (page 12). Cut the squares apart between the stitching lines. Press the seam allowances of the larger unit toward the gold triangles. Reserve the half-square-triangle units for the bonus project.

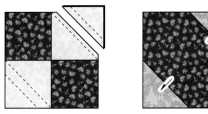

Make 12.

Make 24.
Reserve for bonus project.

3. Repeat step 2 for the remaining corners of the large units, using a gold square on one corner and a blue-and-green half-square-triangle unit from step 1 on the other corner. Be careful to place the half-square-triangle units correctly, with the green half in the lower-left position of six units and in the upper-right position of the remaining six units as shown. This will result in two color options. Square up the units to 6½" x 6½".

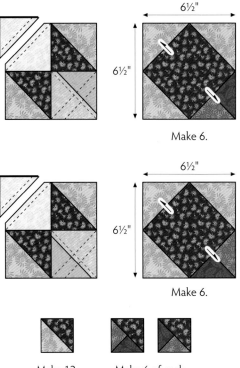

Make 6.

Make 6.

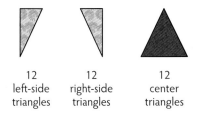

Make 12.   Make 6 of each.

Reserve for bonus project.

Making the Block Triangle Units

Here's what you need:

| 12 left-side triangles | 12 right-side triangles | 12 center triangles |

1. With right sides together, stitch a gold left-side triangle to the left edge of a red center triangle as shown. Press the seam allowances open. Sew a gold right-side triangle to the right edge of the triangle. Press the seam allowances open. Repeat with the remaining center triangles. Square up the units to 3½" x 3½", making sure the outside points of the triangle base end at the corners and the top point is ¼" from the unit top edge.

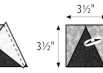

Make 12.

2. Sew the green 3½" squares to the bottom of six triangle units from step 1. Press the seam allowances toward the squares. Repeat with the blue 3½" squares and the remaining triangle units.

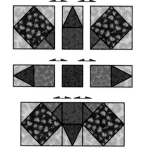

Make 6 of each.

Making the Blocks

Lay out two of each block corner unit, two blue triangle units, two green triangle units, and one red 3½" square into three rows of three units each as shown. Be careful that the corner units are positioned correctly. Join the units in each row. Press the seam allowances open. Join the rows. Press the seam allowances open. Repeat to make a total of three blocks. The blocks should measure 15½" x 15½".

Make 3.

Assembling the Table-Runner Center

Sew the blocks together to make one vertical row. Press the seam allowances open.

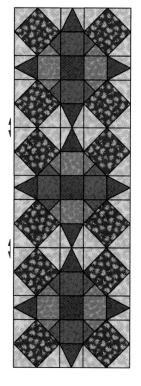

Adding the Borders

Here's what you need:

1 square, 4½"

1 square, 4½"

2 squares, 4"

1. Layer the green 4½" square with the blue 4½" square, right sides together. Stitch diagonally across the pair of squares, ¼" from each side of the points using the gray band alignment on the Clearly Perfect Angles template. Cut the squares apart between the two stitching lines. Press the seam allowances toward the blue triangles. Trim each half-square-triangle unit to 4" x 4".

Make 2.

2. With right sides together, layer the units from step 1 with the brown squares as shown. Stitch diagonally across each square, ¼" from each side of the points as you did in step 1. This will result in two color options. Press the seam allowances open. Square up these units to 3½" x 3½". Set aside these units for the outer border.

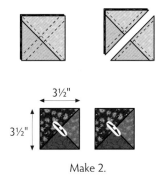

Make 2.

3. Join one of the two pieces left over from cutting the brown 1½" x 17½" strips to one of the brown 1½" x 42" strips. Repeat to make a total of two pieced strips. Trim each of these strips to 1½" x 45½". Refer to the assembly diagram at right to sew these strips to the long sides of the table-runner center. Press the seam allowances toward the border strips. Sew the brown 1½" x 17½" inner-border strips to the short sides of the table-runner center. Press the seam allowances toward the border strips.

4. Join one of the two pieces left over from cutting the green 3½" squares to one of the green 3½" x 42" strips. Repeat to make a total of two pieced strips.

Trim each of these strips to 3½" x 47½". Referring to the diagram, sew these strips to the long sides of the table-runner top. Press the seam allowances toward the outer-border strips. Sew the units from step 2 to the ends of each blue 3½" x 17½" rectangle, making sure the blue triangles are next to the blue rectangles. Press the seam allowances toward the rectangles. Join these strips to the short edges of the table-runner top. Press the seam allowances toward the inner-border strips.

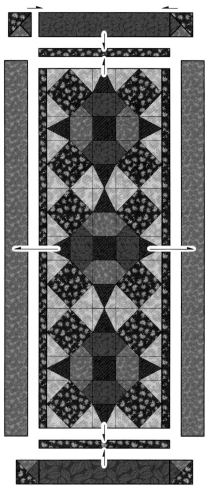

Table-runner assembly

Finishing

For information on how to finish a quilt, including layering, basting, quilting, binding, and more, go to ShopMartingale.com/HowtoQuilt for free downloadable instructions. Use the brown 2¼"-wide strips to bind the table-runner edges.

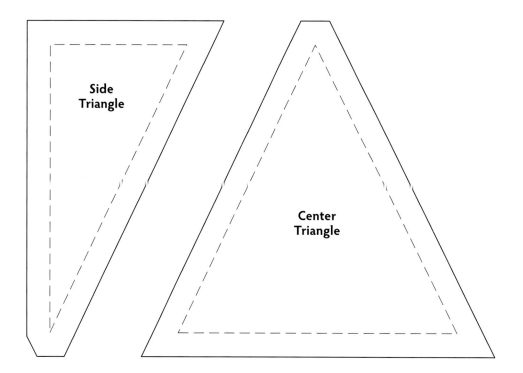

Side Triangle

Center Triangle

BONUS PROJECT:

Sweeten the Pot

Stir the leftovers into the pot and enjoy this appetizing concoction.

Finished Table Topper: 16½" x 16½"

Materials

36 reserved gold-and-brown bonus units from "Split Pea Soup" (page 21)

12 reserved brown-green-and-blue bonus units from "Split Pea Soup"

Leftover green, blue, and brown prints from "Split Pea Soup"

⅝ yard of fabric for backing

20" x 20" square of batting

Cutting

From the remaining green print, cut:
2 rectangles, 2½" x 8½"

From the remaining blue print, cut:
2 rectangles, 2½" x 8½"

From the remaining brown print, cut:
2 strips, 2¼" x 42"

Assembling the Table-Topper Center

1. Press the seam allowances of the reserved bonus units open. Square up the units to 2½" x 2½", making sure all the outside points end at the corners.

Make 36.   Make 6 of each.

2. Lay out seven gold-and-brown units and one each of the brown-green-and-blue units into three rows of three units each. Sew the units in each row together. Press the seam allowances open. Sew the rows together. Press the seam allowances open. Repeat to make a total of four units. The units should measure 6½" x 6½".

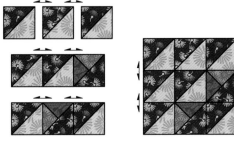

Make 4.

3. Lay out the units from step 2 into two rows of two units each, rotating the units in each row as shown. Sew the units in each row together. Press the seam allowances open. Sew the rows together. Press the

seam allowances open. The table-topper center should measure 12½" x 12½".

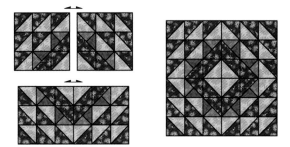

Adding the Borders

1. Referring to the assembly diagram below, join gold-and-brown half-square-triangle units to the ends of each blue rectangle as shown. Press the seam allowances open. Join these border strips to the sides of the table-topper center, making sure the half-square-triangle units are positioned correctly. Press the seam allowances open.

2. Join gold-and-brown half-square-triangle units to the ends of each green rectangle as shown. Press the seam allowances open. Add brown-green-and-blue units to the ends of these strips, paying careful attention to the placement of the colors. Press the seam allowances open. Join these strips to the top and bottom of the table-topper center, paying careful attention to color placement. Press the seam allowances open.

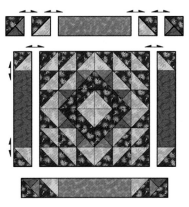

Table-topper assembly

Finishing

For information on how to finish a quilt, including layering, basting, quilting, binding, and more, go to ShopMartingale.com/HowtoQuilt for free downloadable instructions. Use the brown 2¼"-wide strips to bind the table-topper edges.

Prairie Rose

The prairie rose *(Rosa arkansana)* is described as
"a delicate bloom in the midst of the vast, open prairie,"
an image I tried to capture with this lovely wall hanging.

Finished Wall Hanging: 20½" x 20½" • Finished Block: 6" x 6"

Pieced by Kari Carr; quilted by Rosalie Davenport

Materials

Yardage is based on 42"-wide fabric.

½ yard of gray print for blocks, sashing, and outer border

Fat quarter (18" x 22") of cream floral for blocks,
   Dresden Plate appliqué, and prairie points

Fat quarter of blue print for blocks, Dresden Plate
   appliqué, and prairie points

Fat quarter of pink print for blocks, Dresden Plate
   appliqué, and prairie points

Fat quarter of red print for inner border and Dresden
   Plate center appliqué

Fat quarter of blue-and-cream striped fabric for binding

⅔ yard of fabric for backing

25" x 25" piece of batting

Clearly Perfect Angles template

Template plastic

Cutting

*After cutting, reserve all leftovers except the blue-and-
cream striped fabric for the bonus project.*

From the gray print, cut:

1 strip, 6½" x 42"; crosscut into:
- 4 squares, 6½" x 6½"
- 2 rectangles, 2" x 6½"
- 1 strip, 2" x 14"

2 strips, 3" x 42"; crosscut *each strip* into:
- 1 strip, 3" x 16" (2 total)
- 1 strip, 3" x 21" (2 total)

From the blue print, cut:

2 strips, 2½" x 18"; crosscut into:
- 4 squares, 2½" x 2½"
- 4 rectangles, 2½" x 5"

2 strips, 3½" x 18"; crosscut into 8 squares, 3½" x 3½"

From the pink print, cut:

2 strips, 2½" x 18"; crosscut into:
- 4 squares, 2½" x 2½"
- 4 rectangles, 2½" x 5"

2 strips, 3½" x 18"; crosscut into 8 squares, 3½" x 3½"

From the cream floral, cut:

2 strips, 2½" x 18"; crosscut into:
- 4 squares, 2½" x 2½"
- 4 rectangles, 2½" x 5"

3 strips, 3½" x 18"; crosscut into 12 squares, 3½" x 3½"

From the red print, cut:

4 strips, 1½" x 18"; crosscut into:
- 2 strips, 1½" x 14"
- 2 strips, 1½" x 16"

From the blue-and-cream striped fabric, cut:

Enough 2¼"-wide bias strips to equal 100" when pieced
   together

Assembling the Quilt Center

Here's what you need:

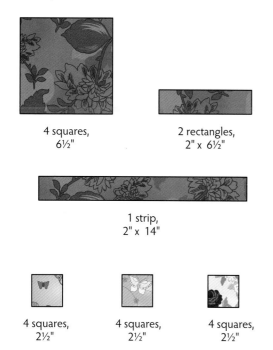

4 squares,
6½"

2 rectangles,
2" x 6½"

1 strip,
2" x 14"

4 squares,
2½"

4 squares,
2½"

4 squares,
2½"

1. With right sides together, place one blue, one cream floral, and one pink square on three corners of each gray square in the order shown. Stitch diagonally from corner to corner as shown, using the basic center alignment (page 7) on the Clearly Perfect Angles template (CPA). Stitch ⅝" from each of the first stitching lines as shown, aligning the corners of the squares with the dotted seam guide on the CPA (page 12).

2. Cut the squares on each corner apart between the seam lines. Press the seam allowances on the block corners toward the triangles. Reserve the half-square-triangle units for the bonus project.

Make 4.

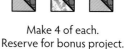

Make 4 of each.
Reserve for bonus project.

3. Sew a square from step 2 to each long side of a gray 2" x 6½" rectangle. Press the seam allowances toward the gray rectangle. Repeat to make a total of two units.

Make 2.

4. Sew the units from step 3 to the long sides of the gray 2" x 14" strip. Press the seam allowances toward the gray strip.

5. Sew the red 1½" x 14" strips to the sides of the joined block unit. Press the seam allowances toward the red strips. Sew the red 1½" x 16" strips to the top and bottom of the block unit. Press the seam allowances toward the strips.

Making the Prairie-Points Border

Here's what you need:

| 8 squares, 3½" | 8 squares, 3½" | 12 squares, 3½" |

1. Press each square in half, wrong sides together. Bring the outer corners of the folded edge to the raw edge, just shy of the center, to create a triangle. Press. This is the right side of the prairie points.

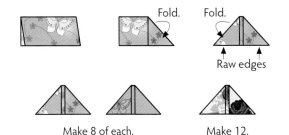

Fold. Fold.

Raw edges

Make 8 of each.   Make 12.

2. With right sides together (folded edge of the prairie points facing the right side of the quilt center), alternate two pink and two blue prairie points along one edge of the red quilt-center border. The points should be facing the center of the quilt. The outer points should begin ⅛" from the ends of the border strips, with approximately ⅝" between the remaining points.

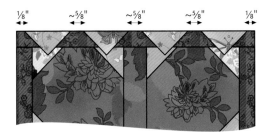

⅛"   ~⅝"   ~⅝"   ~⅝"   ⅛"

3. Layer three cream floral prairie points along the same edge, arranging them between the pink and blue prairie points. Baste close to the edge of each side to hold the prairie points in place.

4. Repeat steps 2 and 3 on each side of the quilt top.
5. Join the gray 3" x 16" strips to opposite sides of the quilt top, stitching through all the layers. Press the seam allowances toward the center while pressing the prairie points toward the gray border. Join the gray 3" x 21" border strips to the top and bottom of the quilt center, stitching through all the layers. Press as before.

Quilt assembly

Appliquéing the Dresden Plate

Here's what you need:

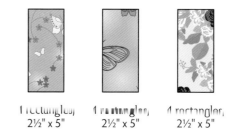

1 rectangle, 2½" x 5"   1 rectangle, 2½" x 5"   4 rectangles, 2½" x 5"

1. Trace the Dresden Plate petal and circle patterns on page 33 onto template plastic and cut them out.
2. Press the rectangles in half lengthwise, right sides together. Stitch ¼" from one short end of each rectangle, securing the stitches at each end. Carefully trim the folded corner on the diagonal near the stitching. Turn and press each rectangle to form folded points at the stitched end, making sure they are square and level.

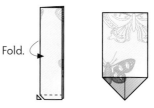

Fold.

3. Lay the petal template on the wrong side of a rectangle unit from step 2. With the points matched, cut away the excess fabric on each long diagonal side and the short end of the template. Repeat with the remaining rectangle units to make the petal pieces.

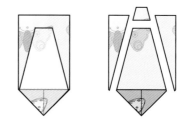

4. Join the petal pieces into a circle by sewing the long raw edges together, carefully matching folded edges and watching color placement. Press all seam allowances in one direction.

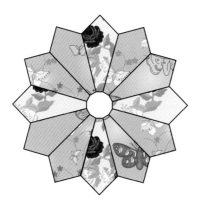

5. Center the Dresden Plate appliqué on the quilt center. Appliqué the outer edges in place using your preferred method, referring to the appliquéing information found at ShopMartingale.com/HowtoQuilt if needed. Use the circle template to

prepare a circle piece from the remaining red fabric. Appliqué it to the center of the Dresden Plate.

Finishing

For information on how to finish a quilt, including layering, basting, quilting, binding, and more, go to ShopMartingale.com/HowtoQuilt for free downloadable instructions. Use the blue-and-cream 2¼"-wide bias strips to bind the quilt edges.

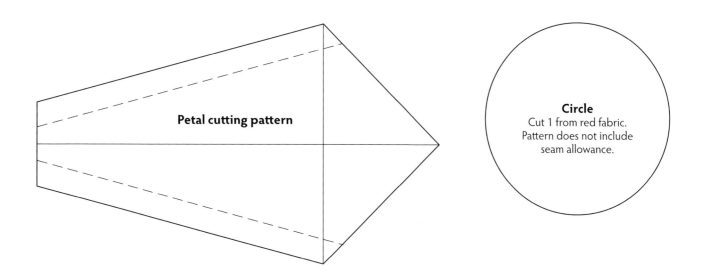

Petal cutting pattern

Circle
Cut 1 from red fabric.
Pattern does not include
seam allowance.

BONUS PROJECT:

A Bed of Roses

With every rose comes the thorns. Use the fallen petals from the "Prairie Rose" wall hanging for a sweet pincushion— a perfect place for keeping your pins and needles.

Finished Pincushion: 3" x 4" x 1½"

Materials

12 reserved bonus units from "Prairie Rose" (page 28)
Leftover fabrics from "Prairie Rose"
5" x 15" rectangle of heavyweight fusible interfacing
Chalk pencil
Seam sealant
Crushed walnut shells (available at pet supply stores) or filling of your choice

Cutting

From the remaining gray print, cut:
1 rectangle, 3½" x 4½"

From *each* of the remaining blue print, pink print, and cream floral, cut:
2 squares, 2" x 2" (6 total)

From the remaining red print, cut:
1 strip, 2" x 14½"

From the heavyweight fusible interfacing, cut:
1 rectangle, 2¾" x 3¾"
1 strip, 1¼" x 13¾"

Assembling the Pincushion

1. Press the seam allowances of the reserved bonus units open. Square up the units to 1½" x 1½", making sure all the outside points end at the corners.

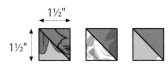

Make 4 of each.

2. Join the bonus units into three rows of four units each, with like colors in each row. Press the seam allowances open. Join the rows. Press the seam allowances open. The pincushion top should measure 3½" x 4½".

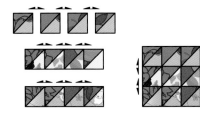

3. Center and fuse the interfacing rectangle to the wrong side of the gray rectangle. Center and fuse the interfacing strip to the wrong side of the red strip.

4. Using the chalk pencil, make a mark ¼" in from each corner on the wrong sides of the interfaced gray rectangle and the pieced top. Make marks as indicated on the wrong side of the interfaced red strip, ¼" from the edges.

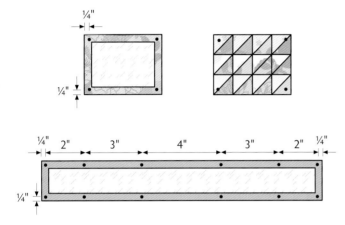

5. Refer to step 1 of "Making the Prairie-Points Border" (page 31) to make prairie points from the blue, pink, and cream floral squares.

Make 2 of each.

6. On one edge of the right side of the red strip, center a cream floral prairie point between each of the markings that are 3" apart. Place the prairie points right side up with the point toward the center of the strip. Place one blue and one pink prairie point between the dots that are 4" apart, spacing them so they overlap and are approximately ⅜" in from the markings. Baste the prairie points in place. Carefully tack the prairie points to the strip so that they'll lie flat when finished.

7. Stitch the short ends of the red strip, right sides together. Press the seam allowances open. Position and baste the remaining blue and pink prairie points in the same manner as you did in step 6; tack into place.

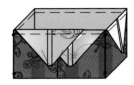

8. Carefully clip into the seam allowance up to but not through the corner markings. With right sides together, pin the edge of the red strip that has the prairie points to the pieced top, matching the marks. Stitch the top to the strip, decreasing the stitch length as you sew around each corner. Leave the needle in the down position when turning to stitch the new side.

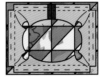

9. In the same manner, stitch the interfaced gray bottom piece to the raw edges of the red strip, leaving an opening along one edge for turning and filling the pincushion. Put a drop of seam sealant at each clipped corner. Turn the pincushion right side out and carefully press the seams.

Leave open for turning.

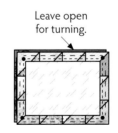

10. Fill the pincushion to the desired plumpness with crushed walnut shells or other filling material. Neatly stitch the seam opening closed.

Heavenly Days

Stars and elegance combine in this bed runner that
will have you exclaiming, "Oh, my heavenly days!"

Finished Bed Runner: 92½" x 26½"

Finished Center Block: 24" x 24" • **Finished End Blocks:** 18" x 18"

Designed by Kari Carr; pieced by Faye Kempfer; quilted by Rosalie Davenport

Materials

Yardage is based on 42"-wide fabric.

2 yards of brown small-scale floral for blocks and
background

1⅓ yards of brown medium-scale floral for blocks
and binding

⅞ yard of gold print for blocks

¾ yard of blue small-scale print for blocks

½ yard of blue leaf print for blocks

2¾ yards of fabric for backing

32" x 98" piece of batting

Clearly Perfect Angles template

Cutting

From the brown medium-scale floral, cut:

3 strips, 6½" x 42"; crosscut into:
- 8 squares, 6½" x 6½"
- 4 rectangles, 6½" x 9½"

7 strips, 2¼" x 42"

From the gold print, cut:

6 strips, 3½" x 42"; crosscut into:
- 52 squares, 3½" x 3½"
- 4 rectangles, 3½" x 6½"

1 strip, 4" x 42"; crosscut into 8 squares, 4" x 4"

From the blue leaf print, cut:

3 strips, 3½" x 42"; crosscut into:
- 8 rectangles, 3½" x 6½"
- 8 squares, 3½" x 3½"

4 squares, 4" x 4"

From the blue small-scale print, cut:

1 strip, 2½" x 42"; crosscut into 12 squares, 2½" x 2½"

1 strip, 6½" x 42"; crosscut into:
- 4 squares, 6½" x 6½"
- 2 squares, 4½" x 4½"

2 strips, 3½" x 42"; crosscut into 18 squares, 3½" x 3½"

From the brown small-scale floral, cut:

4 strips, 1½" x 42"; crosscut into:
- 2 strips, 1½" x 24½"
- 8 rectangles, 1½" x 2½"
- 48 squares, 1½" x 1½"

2 strips, 2½" x 42"; crosscut into:
- 4 rectangles, 2½" x 12½"
- 8 squares, 2½" x 2½"

6 strips, 4½" x 42"; crosscut into:
- 2 strips, 4½" x 26½"
- 4 strips, 4½" x 18½"
- 8 rectangles, 3½" x 4½"
- 4 squares, 4" x 4"

2 strips, 3½" x 42"; crosscut into 14 squares, 3½" x 3½"

2 strips, 7½" x 42"; crosscut into 4 rectangles, 7½" x 12½"

Making the Center Star Block

This block is made by assembling several units. Pay close attention to the color placement in each of these units so that your center star will "pop."

Unit A
Here's what you need:

4 squares,   8 squares,
6½"   3½"

1. With right sides together, place a gold square on one corner of each brown medium-scale floral square. Stitch diagonally from corner to corner as shown, using the basic center alignment (page 7) on the Clearly Perfect Angles template (CPA). Stitch ⅝" from the first stitching line as shown, aligning the corners of the squares with the dotted seam guide on the CPA (page 12). Cut the squares apart between the two stitching lines. Press the seam allowances of the A units toward the gold triangles. Reserve the half-square-triangle units for the bonus project.

Make 4.

Make 4.
Reserve for bonus project.

2. Repeat step 1 on the adjacent corner of each A unit. The A units should measure 6½" x 6½".

Unit A.
Make 4.

Make 4.
Reserve for bonus project.

Unit B
Here's what you need:

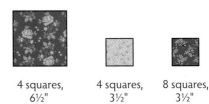

4 squares,   4 squares,   8 squares,
6½"   3½"   3½"

1. With right sides together, place blue leaf-print squares on opposite corners of each brown medium-scale floral square. Stitch diagonally from corner to corner as shown, using the basic center alignment on the CPA. Stitch ⅝" from the first stitching line as shown, aligning the corners of the squares with the dotted seam guide on the CPA.

Cut the squares apart between the two stitching lines. Press the seam allowances of the B units toward the blue triangles. Reserve the half-square-triangle units for the bonus project.

Make 4.

Make 8.
Reserve for bonus project.

2. With right sides together, place a gold square on one of the remaining corners of each unit from step 1. Stitch diagonally from corner to corner as shown, using the basic center alignment on the CPA. Stitch ⅝" from the first stitching line as shown, aligning the corners of the squares with the dotted seam guide on the CPA. Cut the squares apart between the two stitching lines. Press the seam allowances of the B units toward the gold triangles. The units should measure 6½" x 6½". Reserve the half-square-triangle units for the bonus project.

Unit B.
Make 4.

Make 4.
Reserve for bonus project.

Unit C
Here's what you need:

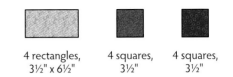

4 rectangles, 3½" x 6½"   4 squares, 3½"   4 squares, 3½"

1. With right sides together, place a blue small-scale print square on the left end of each gold rectangle. Stitch diagonally from corner to corner as shown, using the basic center alignment on the CPA. Stitch ⅝" from the first stitching line as shown, aligning the corners of the squares with the dotted seam guide on the CPA. Cut the pieces apart between the two stitching lines. Reserve the half-square-triangle units for the bonus project.

Make 4.

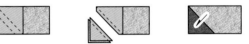

Make 4.
Reserve for bonus project.

2. Repeat step 1, sewing the brown squares to the opposite end of each C unit. Press the seam allowances of the C units toward the brown triangles. The units should measure 6½" x 3½". Reserve the half-square-triangle units for the bonus project.

Unit C.
Make 4.

Make 4.
Reserve for bonus project.

Units D, E, F, and G

Here's what you need:

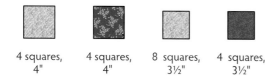

| 4 squares, 4" | 4 squares, 4" | 8 squares, 3½" | 4 squares, 3½" |

1. Layer each blue leaf print square with a gold 4" square, right sides together. Stitch diagonally across each pair of squares, ¼" from each side of the points using the gray band alignment (page 9) on the CPA. Cut the squares apart between the two stitching lines. Press the seam allowances toward the blue triangles. Square up each half-square-triangle unit to 3½" x 3½", making sure all the outside points end at the corners.

Make 8.

2. Join a gold 3½" square to each blue small-scale floral square. Press the seam allowances toward the blue squares. Add a half-square-triangle unit from step 1 to the gold square of each unit, rotating the units as shown to make two each of units D and E. Press the seam allowances toward the gold squares. The units should measure 9½" x 3½".

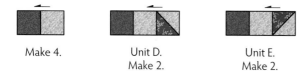

| Make 4. | Unit D.
Make 2. | Unit E.
Make 2. |

3. Sew a gold 3½" square to the remaining half-square-triangle units from step 1 as shown to make two each of units F and G. Press the seam allowances toward the gold squares. The units should measure 6½" x 3½".

| Unit F
Make 2. | Unit G
Make 2. |

Unit H

Here's what you need:

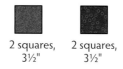

| 2 squares, 3½" | 2 squares, 3½" |

1. Layer each blue small-scale floral square with a brown small-scale floral square, right sides together. Stitch diagonally across each pair of squares, ¼" from each side of the points using the gray band alignment on the CPA. Cut the squares apart between the two stitching lines. Press the seam allowances toward the brown triangles. Trim each half-square-triangle unit to 3½" x 3½".

Make 4.

2. Arrange the half-square-triangle units from step 1 into two rows of two units each, rotating the units as shown. Pay attention to color placement so that the center star is formed correctly. Sew the units in each row together. Press the seam allowances as shown. Sew the rows together to make a pinwheel unit. Fan the seam allowances at the intersection to reduce bulk. To fan the seam allowances, remove the stitching above the horizontal seam allowance, and then press the seam allowances in opposite directions. The unit should measure 6½" x 6½".

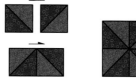

Unit H.
Make 1.

Assembling the Center Block

1. Sew the F and G units to the B units as shown. Make two of each. Press the seam allowances toward the B units. Add the D and E units to the top of these units as shown. Press the seam allowances open. The unit should measure 9½" x 9½".

Make 2.

Make 2.

2. Sew a C unit to the bottom of each A unit.

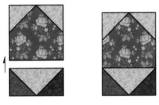

Make 4.

3. Lay out the units from steps 1 and 2 with unit H into three horizontal rows. Sew the units in each row together. Press the seam allowances open. Sew the rows together. Press the seam allowances open. The block should measure 24½" x 24½".

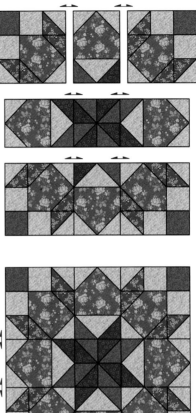

Making the End Blocks

These blocks are also made by assembling several units. Pay close attention to the color placement in each of these units to achieve the desired star effect.

Unit A

Here's what you need:

4 rectangles, 6½" x 9½"   8 squares, 3½"   8 squares, 3½"

1. With right sides together, place a gold square on one corner of each brown medium-scale floral rectangle. Stitch diagonally from corner to corner as shown, using the basic center alignment on the CPA. Stitch ⅝" from the first stitching line as shown, aligning the corners of the squares with the dotted seam guide on the CPA. Cut the squares apart between the two stitching lines. Press the seam allowances of the A units toward the gold triangles. Reserve the half-square-triangle units for the bonus project. Repeat on the adjacent corner with the remaining gold squares.

Make 4.

Make 8.
Reserve for bonus project.

2. Repeat step 1 on the remaining two corners of the brown rectangles using the blue small-scale print squares. The units should measure 6½" x 9½".

 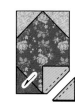 

Unit A.
Make 4.

Make 8.
Reserve for bonus project.

Unit B
Here's what you need:

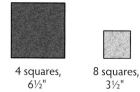

4 squares,
6½"

8 squares,
3½"

1. With right sides together, place a gold square on one corner of each blue small-scale print square. Stitch diagonally from corner to corner as shown, using the basic center alignment on the CPA. Stitch ⅝" from the first stitching line as shown, aligning the corners of the squares with the dotted seam guide on the CPA. Cut the squares apart between the two stitching lines. Press the seam allowances of the B units toward the gold triangles. Reserve the half-square-triangle units for the bonus project.

Make 4.

Make 4.
Reserve for bonus project.

2. Repeat step 1 on the adjacent corner of each B unit. The B units should measure 6½" x 6½".

Unit B.
Make 4.

Make 4.
Reserve for bonus project.

Units C and D

Here's what you need:

4 squares,
4"

4 squares,
4"

8 squares,
3½"

1. Layer each brown small-scale floral square with a gold 4" square, right sides together. Stitch diagonally across each pair of squares, ¼" from each side of the points using the gray band alignment on the CPA. Cut the squares apart between the two stitching lines. Press the seam allowances toward the brown triangles. Square up each half-square-triangle unit to 3½" x 3½", making sure all the outside points end at the corners.

3½"

3½"

Make 8.

2. Sew a gold 3½" square to each half-square-triangle unit from step 1 as shown to make two each of units C and D. Press the seam allowances toward the gold squares. The units should measure 6½" x 3½".

Unit C.
Make 4.

Unit D.
Make 4.

Units E and F

Here's what you need:

8 rectangles,
3½" x 6½"

8 squares,
3½"

8 squares,
3½"

1. With right sides together, place a gold square on the left end of each blue leaf-print rectangle. Stitch diagonally from corner to corner as shown, using the basic center alignment on the CPA. Stitch ⅝" from the first stitching line as shown, aligning the corners of the squares with the dotted seam guide on the CPA. Cut the squares apart between the two stitching lines. Press the seam allowances of the E units toward the gold triangles. Reserve the half-square-triangle units for the bonus project.

Make 4.

Make 4.
Reserve for bonus project.

2. Repeat step 1 to sew a brown square to the opposite end of each E unit, being careful to stitch in the direction shown. Press the seam allowances of the E units toward the brown triangles. The E units should measure 6½" x 3½". Reserve the half-square-triangle units for the bonus project.

Unit E.
Make 4.

Make 4.
Reserve for bonus project.

3. Repeat steps 1 and 2 with the remaining pieces, reversing the placement of the gold and brown squares as shown, to make the F units.

Unit F.
Make 4.

Make 4 of each.
Reserve for bonus project.

Assembling the End Blocks

1. Sew a C unit to each E unit as shown. Press the seam allowances open. Sew a D unit to each F unit as shown. Press the seam allowances open.

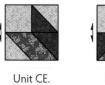

Unit CE.
Make 4.

Unit DF.
Make 4.

2. Lay out two CE units and two DF units from step 1 with two A units and two B units to form three vertical rows as shown. Sew the units in each row together. Press the seam allowances open. Sew the rows together. Press the seam allowances open. Repeat to make a total of two blocks. The blocks should measure 18½" x 18½".

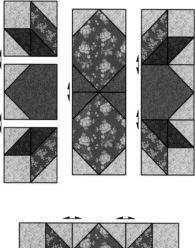

Make 2.

Making the Diamond Setting Units

Here's what you need:

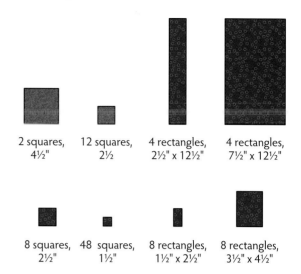

2 squares, 4½"

12 squares, 2½

4 rectangles, 2½" x 12½"

4 rectangles, 7½" x 12½"

8 squares, 2½"

48 squares, 1½"

8 rectangles, 1½" x 2½"

8 rectangles, 3½" x 4½"

1. Place brown small-scale floral 2½" squares on opposite corners of each blue small-scale print 4½" square. Stitch diagonally from corner to corner as shown, using the basic center alignment on the CPA. Trim ¼" from the stitching lines and press the seam allowances toward the brown triangles.

Make 2.

2. Repeat step 1 on the remaining corners of the blue square to make two large square-in-a-square units. The units should measure 4½" x 4½".

Make 2.

3. Repeat steps 1 and 2 with the blue small-scale print 2½" squares and the brown small-scale floral 1½" squares to make 12 small square-in-a-square units. The units should measure 2½" x 2½".

Make 12.

4. Join two small square-in-a-square units. Press the seam allowances open. Repeat to make a total of four units. The units should measure 2½" x 4½".

Make 4.

5. Sew the brown small-scale floral 3½" x 4½" rectangles to opposite sides of each unit from step 4. Press the seam allowances toward the rectangles.

Make 4.

6. Sew the brown small-scale floral 1½" x 2½" rectangles to the top and bottom of each remaining small square-in-a-square unit. Press the seam allowances toward the rectangles.

Make 4.

7. Sew the units from step 6 to opposite sides of each large square-in-a-square unit. Press the seam allowances open. The units should measure 8½" x 4½".

Make 2.

8. Sew the units from step 5 to the top and bottom of each unit from step 7. Press the seam allowances open. Join the brown small-scale floral 2½" x 12½" rectangles to opposite sides of these units. Press the seam allowances toward the rectangles.

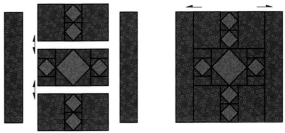

Make 2.

9. Sew the brown small-scale floral 7½" x 12½" rectangles to the top and bottom of each unit from step 8. Press the seam allowances toward the rectangles. The units should measure 12½" x 26½".

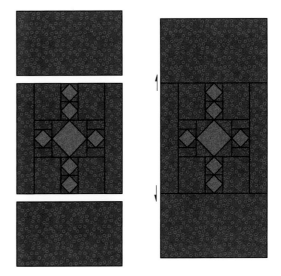

Make 2.

Assembling the Bed-Runner Top

1. Referring to the assembly diagram on page 46, sew the brown small-scale floral 4½" x 18½" strips to the top and bottom of each of the end blocks. Press the seam allowances toward the strips. Join a brown small-scale floral 4½" x 26½" strip to the outside edge of each end block. Press the seam allowances toward the strips.

2. Sew the brown small-scale floral 1½" x 24½" strips to the top and bottom of the center block. Press the seam allowances toward the strips.

3. Lay out the end blocks, center blocks, and setting units and sew them together as shown. Press the seam allowances toward the setting units.

Finishing

For information on how to finish a quilt, including layering, basting, quilting, binding, and more, go to ShopMartingale.com/HowtoQuilt for free downloadable instructions. Use the brown medium-scale floral 2¼"-wide strips to bind the bed-runner edges.

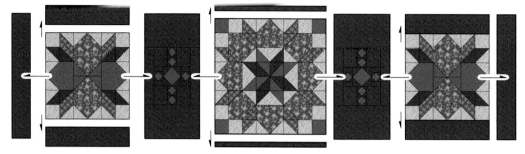

Bed-runner assembly

BONUS PROJECT:

Heaven's Sake

For heaven's sake, why not continue the radiance with this small piece that can be displayed on a dresser or table?

Finished Table Runner: 16½" x 28½"

Materials

68 reserved bonus units from "Heavenly Days" (page 36)

Leftover brown small-scale floral, blue small-scale print, and brown medium-scale floral fabrics from "Heavenly Days"

⅔ yard of fabric for backing

20" x 32" piece of batting

Cutting

From the remaining brown small-scale floral, cut:
4 rectangles, 2½" x 4½"

From the remaining blue small-scale print, cut:
2 rectangles, 2½" x 12½"
2 strips, 2½" x 24½"

From the remaining brown medium-scale floral, cut:
3 strips, 2¼" x 42"

Assembling the Table-Runner Top

1. Press the seam allowances of the reserved bonus units open. Square up the units to 2½" x 2½", making sure all the outside points end at the corners.

Make 20.   Make 12.   Make 4.

Make 8 of each.

2. Referring to the assembly diagram at right, arrange the half-square-triangle units and brown small-scale floral rectangles into 12 rows as shown. Sew the units in each row together. Press the seam allowances open. Sew the rows together. Press the seam allowances open.

3. Sew the blue 2½" x 24½" border strips to the long edges of the center unit. Press the seam allowances toward the border strips. Add the remaining four half-square-triangle units to the ends of the blue 2½" x 12½" rectangles. Press the seam allowances

toward the rectangles. Join these strips to the short edges of the center unit. Press the seam allowances toward the table-runner center.

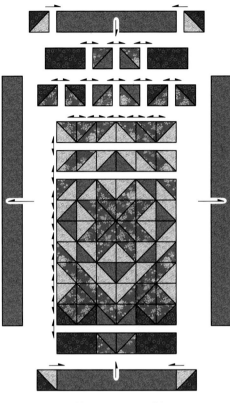

Table-runner assembly

Finishing

For information on how to finish a quilt, including layering, basting, quilting, binding, and more, go to ShopMartingale.com/HowtoQuilt for free downloadable instructions. Use the brown medium-scale floral 2¼"-wide strips to bind the table-runner edges.

Liberty

Take the liberty to scatter this star quilt across a table,
drape it from a railing, or simply fling it over a chair.
Single stylized blocks in this unique setting truly shine.

Finished Quilt: 45½" x 59½" • Finished Block: 14" x 14"

Pieced by Kari Carr; quilted by Penny Miller

Materials

Yardage is based on 42"-wide fabric.

1½ yards of cream multicolored print for outer border

1¼ yards of dark-blue print for blocks, appliqué, and
binding

1⅛ yards of red print #1 for block centers, inner border,
and appliqué

⅞ yard of tan print for block backgrounds

¾ yard of medium-blue print for block frames

⅝ yard of cream-with-blue print for block corners and
inner border

½ yard of red print #2 for block star points

3 yards of fabric for backing

52" x 66" piece of batting

Clearly Perfect Angles template

Cutting

From red print #1, cut:

3 strips, 3½" x 42"; crosscut into 24 squares, 3½" x 3½"

2 strips, 4" x 42"; crosscut into 14 squares, 4" x 4"

1 strip, 14½" x 42"; crosscut into 10 rectangles,
3½" x 14½"

From the dark-blue print, cut:

4 strips, 4" x 42"; crosscut into 36 squares, 4" x 4"

6 strips, 2¼" x 42"

From the tan print, cut:

7 strips, 3½" x 42"; crosscut into:
- 24 squares, 3½" x 3½"
- 24 rectangles, 3½" x 6½"

From red print #2, cut:

3 strips, 4" x 42"; crosscut into 24 squares, 4" x 4"

From the medium-blue print, cut:

2 strips, 2¾" x 42"; crosscut into 24 squares, 2¾" x 2¾"

1 strip, 14½" x 42"; crosscut into:
- 12 strips, 1½" x 14½"
- 12 strips, 1½" x 12½"

From the cream-with-blue print, cut:

4 strips, 3½" x 42"; crosscut into 44 squares, 3½" x 3½"

2 squares, 4" x 4"

**From the *lengthwise grain* of the cream
multicolored print, cut:**

2 strips, 6" x 48½"

2 strips, 6" x 45½"

Making the Star Block Centers

Here's what you need:

12 squares,
4"   12 squares,
4"   24 squares,
3½"

1. Layer each 4" dark-blue square with a 4" red print #1 square, right sides together. Stitch diagonally across each pair of squares, ¼" from each side of the points using the gray band alignment (page 9) on the Clearly Perfect Angles template (CPA). Cut the squares apart between the two stitching lines. Press the seam allowances toward the red triangles. Trim each half-square-triangle unit to 3½" x 3½".

Make 24.

2. Layer each half-square-triangle unit from step 1 with a 3½" red print #1 square, right sides together. Stitch diagonally from corner to corner as shown, using the basic center alignment (page 7) on the CPA. Stitch ⅝" from the first stitching line as shown, aligning the corners of the squares with the dotted seam guide on the CPA (page 12). *Refer to the color placement of the blue and red half-square triangles to determine on which side the ⅝" seam should be sewn.* Cut the squares apart between the two stitching lines. Press the seam allowances of the larger units toward the large red triangle. Trim the larger units to 3½" x 3½". Reserve the smaller units for the bonus project.

Make 24.

Make 24.
Reserve for bonus project.

3. Arrange the larger units from step 2 into two rows of two units each as shown. Sew the units in each row together. Press the seam allowances toward the large red triangles. Sew the rows together. Press the

seam allowances open. The star center units should measure 6½" x 6½".

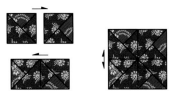

Make 6.

Making the Star Block Points

Here's what you need:

24 squares, 4" 24 squares, 4"

24 rectangles, 3½" x 6½" 24 squares, 3½"

1. Layer each 4" dark-blue square with a 4" red print #2 square, right sides together. Stitch diagonally across each pair of squares, ¼" from each side of the points using the gray band alignment on the CPA. Cut the squares apart between the two stitching lines. Press the seam allowances toward the red triangles. Trim each half-square-triangle unit to 3½" x 3½".

Make 48.

2. Position a half-square-triangle unit on the left end of each tan rectangle so that the red triangle is in the upper corner of the rectangle as shown. Stitch diagonally from corner to corner as shown, using the basic center alignment on the CPA. Stitch ⅝"

from the first stitching lines as shown, aligning the corners of the squares with the dotted seam guide on the CPA. Cut the pieces apart between the two stitching lines. Press the seam allowances of the rectangle units toward the red-and-blue triangles. Reserve the cut-away units for the bonus project.

Make 24.

Make 24.
Reserve for bonus project.

3. Repeat step 2 on the right end of each tan rectangle. Press the seam allowances of the rectangle units toward the red-and-blue triangles. The units should measure 6½" x 3½". Reserve the cut-away units for the bonus project.

Make 24.

Make 24.
Reserve for bonus project.

Assembling the Blocks

Here's what you need:

24 squares, 2¾"   12 strips, 1½" x 12½"   24 squares, 3½"

12 strips, 1½" x 14½"

1. Lay out one center unit, four star point units, and four tan squares into three rows as shown. Join the units in each row. Press the seam allowances of the top and bottom rows toward the squares. Press the seam allowances of the middle row open. Join the rows. Press the seam allowances open. Repeat to make a total of six units. The units should measure 12½" x 12½".

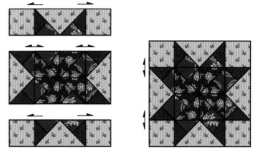

Make 6.

2. Place a 2¾" medium-blue square on each corner of each unit from step 1, right sides together. Stitch diagonally from corner to corner as shown, using the basic center alignment on the CPA. Trim ¼" from the stitching lines and press the seam allowances toward the blue triangles.

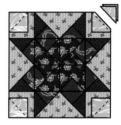 

Make 6.

3. Sew the 1½" x 12½" medium-blue framing strips to the top and bottom of each star unit. Press the seam allowances toward the strips. Add the 1½" x 14½" medium-blue framing strips to the sides of the units. Press the seam allowances toward the strips.

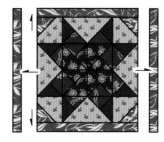

4. Place a cream-with-blue square on each corner of the block, right sides together. Stitch diagonally from corner to corner as shown, using the basic center alignment on the CPA. Stitch ⅝" from the first stitching lines as shown, aligning the corners of the squares with the dotted seam guide on the CPA. Cut the pieces apart between the two stitching lines. Press the seam allowances of the blocks toward the cream-with-blue triangles. Reserve the cut-away units for the bonus project.

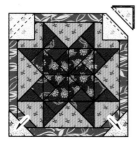 

Make 6.

Make 24.
Reserve for bonus project.

Making the Inner-Border Units

Here's what you need:

10 rectangles,
3½" x 14½"

20 squares, 2 squares, 2 squares,
3½"   4"   4"

1. Place 3½" cream-with-blue squares on the ends of each red rectangle, right sides together. Stitch diagonally from corner to corner as shown, using the basic center alignment on the CPA. Stitch ⅝" from the first stitching lines as shown, aligning the corners of the squares with the dotted seam guide on the CPA. Cut the pieces apart between the two stitching lines. Press the seam allowances of the rectangle units toward the cream triangles. Reserve the half-square-triangle units for the bonus project.

Make 10.

Make 20.
Reserve for bonus project.

2. Layer each 4" red square with a 4" cream-with-blue square, right sides together. Stitch diagonally across each pair of squares, ¼" from each side of the points using the gray band alignment on the CPA. Cut the squares apart between the two stitching lines. Press the seam allowances toward the red triangles. Trim each half-square-triangle unit to 3½" x 3½".

Make 4.

Assembling the Quilt Top

1. Refer to the quilt assembly diagram on page 53 to arrange the blocks into three rows of two blocks each. Sew the blocks in each row together. Press the seam allowances open. Sew the rows together. Press the seam allowances open.

2. Join three red border units end to end as shown. Repeat to make a total of two border strips. Press the seam allowances open. Join these units to the sides of the quilt center. Press the seam allowances open.

3. In the same manner, join two red border units end to end. Repeat to make a total of two border strips. Join the half-square-triangle units from step 2 of "Making the Inner-Border Units" to the ends of each of these border strips. Press the seam allowances open. Join these strips to the top and bottom of the quilt center. Press the seam allowances open.

4. Join the 6" x 48½" cream multicolored strips to the sides of the quilt top. Press the seam allowances toward the outer-border strips. Add the 6" x 45½" cream multicolored strips to the top and bottom edges of the quilt top. Press the seam allowances toward the outer-border strips.

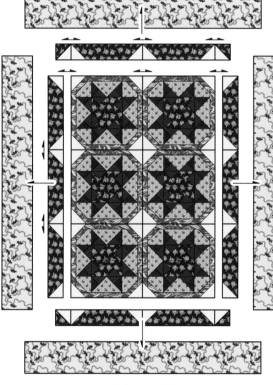

Quilt assembly

Adding the Appliqués

1. Refer to the turned-edge appliquéing information found at ShopMartingale.com/HowtoQuilt and use the patterns (at right) to prepare the appliqué pieces from the fabrics indicated.

2. Center the dark-blue circles on each of the cream-with-blue on-point squares. Stitch each circle in place using your method of choice. Center and appliqué the red crosses over the blue circles.

Finishing

For information on how to finish a quilt, including layering, basting, quilting, binding, and more, go to ShopMartingale.com/HowtoQuilt for free downloadable instructions. Use the 2¼"-wide dark-blue strips to bind the quilt edges.

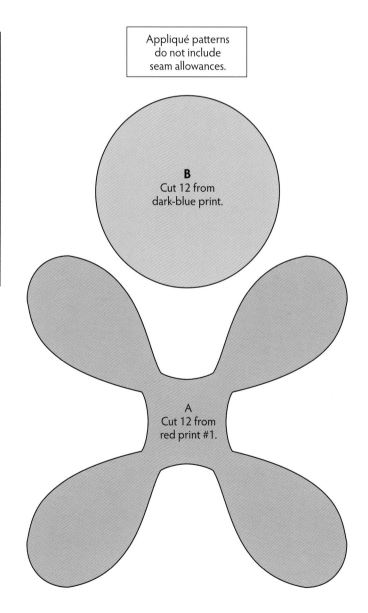

Appliqué patterns do not include seam allowances.

B
Cut 12 from dark-blue print.

A
Cut 12 from red print #1.

How Sweet It Is

Scatterings of stardust mingle in this twinkling quilt as it reminds us of how sweet liberty genuinely is.

Finished Table Topper: 26½" x 30½"

Materials

116 reserved bonus units from "Liberty" (page 48)
Leftover dark-blue, medium-blue, cream-with-blue, and cream multicolored prints from "Liberty"
1 yard of fabric for backing
31" x 35" piece of batting

Cutting

From the remaining medium-blue print, cut:
2 squares, 3" x 3"

From the remaining cream-with-blue print, cut:
2 squares, 3" x 3"

From the *lengthwise grain* of the remaining cream multicolored print, cut:
2 strips, 3½" x 26½"
2 strips, 3½" x 24½"

From the remaining dark-blue print, cut:
3 strips, 2¼" x 42"

Assembling the Table-Topper Top

1. Layer each medium-blue 3" square with a cream-with-blue 3" square, right sides together. Stitch diagonally across each pair of squares, ¼" from each side of the points using the gray band alignment (page 9) on the Clearly Perfect Angles template.

Cut the squares apart between the two stitching lines. Press the seam allowances open. Trim each half-square-triangle unit to 2½" x 2½".

Make 4.

2. Press the seam allowances of the reserved bonus units open. Square up the units to 2½" x 2½".

Make 20.

Make 24 of each.

3. Sew the bonus units and the units from step 1 into pairs as shown. Make the number indicated for each pair. Press the seam allowances open.

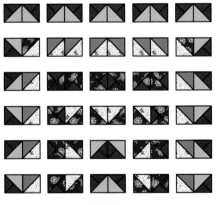

Make 2.   Make 2.   Make 2.   Make 2.

Make 2.   Make 10.   Make 2.   Make 4.

Make 4.   Make 4.   Make 2.   Make 2.

Make 4.   Make 2.   Make 2.   Make 2.

Make 2.   Make 2.   Make 2.   Make 2.

Make 2.   Make 2.

4. Arrange the pairs in six rows as shown. Sew the pairs in each row together. Press the seam allowances open. Sew the rows together. Press the seam allowances open. Repeat to make a total of two units.

Make 2.

5. Referring to the assembly diagram below, sew the units from step 4 together so that they are mirror images of each other. Press the seam allowances open.

6. Sew the cream multicolored 3½" x 24½" strips to the sides of the table-topper center. Press the seam allowances toward the border strips. Sew the cream multicolored 3½" x 26½" strips to the top and bottom of the table-topper center. Press the seam allowances toward the border strips.

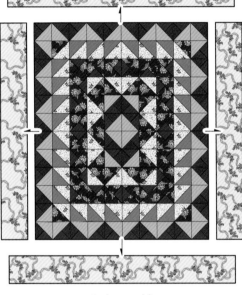

Quilt assembly

Finishing

For information on how to finish a quilt, including layering, basting, quilting, binding, and more, go to ShopMartingale.com/HowtoQuilt for free downloadable instructions. Use the dark-blue 2¼"-wide strips to bind the table-topper edges.

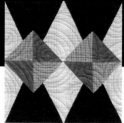

To Sir, with Love

A strikingly unique shape combined with flannel
fabric results in a classic, masculine design. This project
is not for the faint of heart, but it's definitely worth it for the one you love.

Finished Quilt: 75½" x 81½" Finished Block: 6" x 12"

Designed by Kari Carr; pieced by Kari Carr and Faye Kempfer; quilted by Penny Miller

Materials

Yardage is based on 40"-wide flannel fabric.
2½ yards of cream plaid for block centers
2⅓ yards of cream checked fabric for sashing
2⅛ yards of black plaid for border
2 yards of black print for blocks and border corner squares
1⅛ yards of blue checked fabric for blocks
1⅛ yards of blue herringbone print for blocks
1¼ yards of blue striped fabric for bias binding
5⅓ yards of fabric for backing
81" x 87" piece of batting
Clearly Perfect Angles template
Template plastic or Tri-Recs Tools

Cutting

*If you aren't using the Tri-Recs Tools, trace the patterns
on page 62 onto template plastic and cut them out.*

From the black print, cut:
10 strips, 6½" x 42". From the strips, cut:
- 100 right-facing triangles and 100 left-facing triangles (200 triangles total) using the Recs Tool **OR** the side-triangle template
- 4 squares, 6½" x 6½"

From the cream plaid, cut:
15 strips, 6½" x 42". From the strips, cut 100 triangles
using the Tri Tool **OR** the center-triangle template.

From the blue checked fabric, cut:
10 strips, 3½" x 42"; crosscut into 100 squares, 3½" x 3½"

From the blue herringbone print, cut:
10 strips, 3½" x 42"; crosscut into 100 squares,
3½" x 3½"

**From the *lengthwise grain* of the cream checked
fabric, cut:**
2 strips, 2" x 75½"
2 strips, 2" x 66½"
4 strips, 2" x 60½"
4 rectangles, 2" x 6½"

From the *lengthwise grain* of the black plaid, cut:
2 strips, 6½" x 66½"
2 strips, 6½" x 60½"

From the *bias* of the blue striped fabric, cut:
Enough 2¼"-wide strips to equal 325" when sewn
together end to end

Making the Blocks

Here's what you need:

100 left-side   100 right-side   100 center
triangles   triangles   triangles

100 squares,   100 squares,
3½"   3½"

1. With right sides together, stitch a black-print left-side triangle to the left edge of a cream plaid center triangle as shown. Press the seam allowances open. Sew a right-side triangle to the right edge of the center triangle. Press the seam allowances open. Repeat with the remaining center triangles. Square up the units to 6½" x 6½", making sure the outside points of the triangle base end at the corners and the top point is ¼" from the unit top edge.

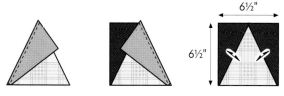

Make 100.

2. With right sides together, place a blue herringbone square on the lower-left corner of each unit from step 1. Stitch diagonally from corner to corner as shown, using the basic center alignment (page 7) on the Clearly Perfect Angles template (CPA). Stitch ⅝" from the first stitching line as shown, aligning the corners of the squares with the dotted seam guide on the CPA (page 12). Cut the pieces apart between the two stitching lines. Press the seam allowances of the large units open. Reserve the cut-away half-square-triangle units for the bonus project.

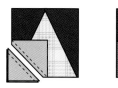

Make 100.

Make 100.
Reserve for bonus project.

3. Repeat step 2 on the lower-right corner of each triangle unit using the blue checked squares. The triangle units should measure 6½" x 6½".

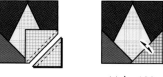

Make 100.

Make 100.
Reserve for bonus project.

4. With right sides together, stitch two triangle units from step 3 together as shown, matching points. Press the seam allowances open. Repeat to make a total of 50 blocks. The blocks should measure 6½" x 12½".

Make 50.

Assembling the Quilt Top

1. Sew 10 blocks together along the long edges to make a row. Press the seam allowances open. Repeat to make a total of five rows.

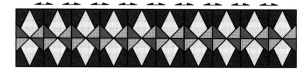

Make 5 rows.

2. Refer to the quilt assembly diagram on page 59 to alternately join the block rows and the four cream checked 2" x 60½" sashing strips. Press the seam allowances toward the sashing strips.

3. Sew a cream checked 2" x 66½" strip to one long edge of each black plaid 6½" x 66½" strip. Press the seam allowances toward the cream strips. Sew the pieced border strips to the sides of the quilt center. Press the seam allowances toward the border strips.

4. Join a cream checked 2" x 6½" rectangle to one side of a black print 6½" square. Press the seam allowances toward the rectangle. Repeat to make a total of four units. Sew the units to the ends of the black plaid 6½" x 60½" strips as shown. Sew a cream checked 2" x 75½" strip to one long edge of each of these pieced strips. Sew the pieced border strips to the top and bottom edges of the quilt top. Press the seam allowances toward the pieced border strips.

Finishing

For information on how to finish a quilt, including layering, basting, quilting, binding, and more, go to ShopMartingale.com/HowtoQuilt for free downloadable instructions. Use the blue striped bias strips to bind the quilt edges.

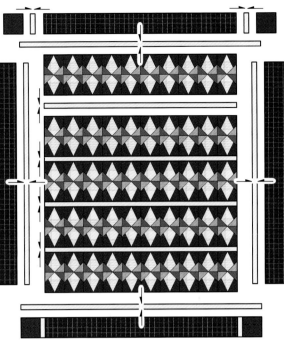

Quilt assembly

BONUS PROJECT:

Head over Heels

Bonus units combine to create a surprising look that would be perfectly stunning hanging on the wall of your guy's den—a small reminder of the love you share. You won't use all of the reserved bonus units from the main project; discard them or save them for another project.

Finished Wall Hanging: 32½" x 36½"

Materials

88 reserved blue checked bonus units from "To Sir, with Love" (page 56)

96 reserved blue herringbone bonus units from "To Sir, with Love"

Leftover cream checked, black plaid, and blue striped fabrics from "To Sir, with Love"

1¼ yards of fabric for backing

36" x 40" piece of batting

Cutting

From the *lengthwise grain* of the remaining cream checked fabric, cut:

3 strips, 1½" x 75"

6 strips, 1½" x 29½"

From the *lengthwise grain* of the remaining black plaid, cut:

2 strips, 4½" x 34½"

2 strips, 4½" x 29½"

From the *bias* of the remaining blue striped fabric, cut:

Enough 2¼"-wide strips to equal 150" when sewn together end to end

Making the Blocks

1. Press the seam allowances of the reserved bonus units open. Square up the units to 2½" x 2½". It is *very* important to trim these pieces so that the 45° angle is maintained on the diagonal of each square and the outside points end at the corners. I recommend marking the seam allowances at the narrowest angles and utilizing the marks on your ruler for accuracy while cutting.

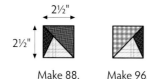

Make 88.　　Make 96.

2. Arrange four blue checked units into two vertical rows of two units each as shown. Sew the units in each row together. Press the seam allowances open. Sew the rows together. Press the seam allowances open. Repeat to make a total of 22 blue checked blocks. Repeat with the blue houndstooth units, arranging the units as shown, to make a total of 24 blocks. The blocks should measure 4½" x 4½".

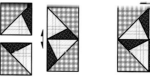

Make 22.

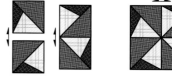

Make 24.

Assembling the Wall-Hanging Top

1. With right sides together and raw edges aligned as shown, place 15 checked blocks and 20 houndstooth blocks on the cream checked 1½" x 75" sashing strips, leaving about 1" of space between the blocks. Sew continuously, making sure to stitch to the points on the blocks.

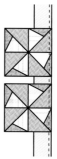

2. Trim the sashing even with the top and bottom edges of each block. Press the seam allowances toward the sashing. The units should measure 5½" x 4½".

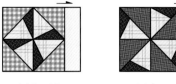

Make 15.　　　Make 20.

3. Sew five blue houndstooth units together side by side as shown. Add one of the remaining houndstooth blocks to the end of the row. Press the seam allowances toward the sashing. Repeat to make a total of four rows. Repeat with the blue checked units to make a total of three rows.

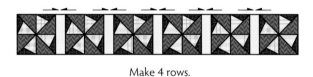

Make 4 rows.

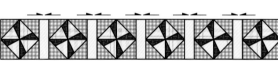

Make 3 rows.

4. Refer to the assembly diagram at right to alternately join the block rows and cream checked 1½" x 29½" sashing strips. Press the seam allowances toward the sashing strips.

5. Add the black plaid 4½" x 34½" border strips to the sides of the quilt center. Press the seam allowances toward the border strips. Sew a blue checked block to each end of the black plaid 4½" x 29½" strips. Press the seam allowances toward the strips. Join these border strips to the top and bottom of the quilt center. Press the seam allowances toward the border strips.

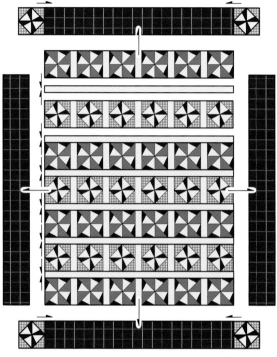

Quilt assembly

Finishing

For information on how to finish the quilt, including layering, basting, quilting, binding, and more, go to ShopMartingale.com/HowtoQuilt for free downloadable instructions. Use the blue striped bias strips to bind the wall-hanging edges.

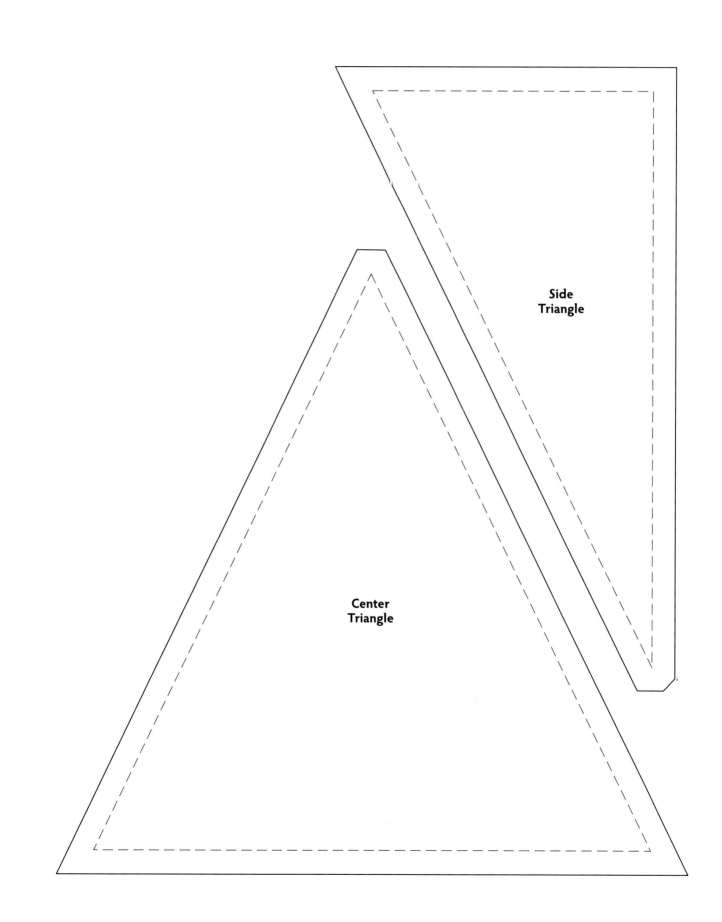

Side
Triangle

Center
Triangle

Acknowledgments

Words seem so inadequate as I try to express the gratitude I feel in my heart. I am very blessed to have friends and family who have not only been supportive of this venture, but have all, in some way, been an inspiration. Thank you from the bottom of my heart.

I could not ask for a better pinner, presser, proofer, etc., etc., etc., than Faye Kempfer. Working with my dear assistant truly made this endeavor twice as nice. Thank you, Miss Faye.

Penny Miller and Rosalie Davenport once again shared their creativeness in the quilting of these projects. Your talent is amazing. Thank you.

Thank you Karen Perry, Rebekah Thompson, and Carri Thompson for your special encouragement and willingness to go those few extra stitches for me.

My appreciation goes to the following companies for graciously providing fabric:

"Prairie Rose" (page 28): "Papillon" by 3 Sisters for Moda Fabrics

"Heavenly Days" (page 36): "The Cocheco Mills Collection" by Judie Rothermel for Marcus Fabrics

"Liberty" (page 48): "Sara's Stash" by Sara Morgan for Blue Hill Fabrics

"To Sir, with Love" (page 56): "Woolies" by Bonnie Sullivan and Maywood Studio

Thank you to the whole team at Martingale, especially Karen Costello Soltys, Mary V. Green, Karen Johnson, and Mary Burns. You are the best! I so appreciate the art department's commitment, led by Paula Schlosser. And finally thanks to Laurie Baker for her patience through all the editing.

I couldn't do this without the love and support of my whole family. You are all so very dear to me! My heart is full because I am married to the most caring, kind, and oh-so-patient man. Thank you, Brian, for being my biggest and most devoted fan. Together we are twice as nice. I love you.

About the Author

Kari Carr has enjoyed working with textiles since she was a little girl. Her mom encouraged her interests in sewing and crafting, and Kari furthered this love in college as she obtained her Home Economics degree.

Her quilt-design company, New Leaf Stitches, began while she was still teaching at her local high school. After she developed the popular notion Clearly Perfect Angles, Kari's company prospered to the point where she was able to leave her teaching position to pursue her passion full-time.

Kari feels blessed to still get her teaching "fix" by teaching quilting across the country. Hearing, "Oh, you're the recycled Home-Ec teacher!" has been an affirmation of why she turned over a *new leaf*. Kari is the author of *Just around the Corner: Quilts with Easy Mitered Borders* (Martingale, 2011) and her work has been featured on the covers of leading quilt magazines in the United States and France. Her company's website, NewLeafStitches.com, features patterns and information about the Clearly Perfect Angles template. Kari also shares a glimpse into her life and business on her blog.

Kari and her husband, Brian, have lived in the beautiful Minnesota lakes country their entire lives. Their world just got twice as nice with the addition of their second granddaughter. Family is one of the many things for which she thanks God daily.